# Little Coffee Shop Poems

Claire Gifford

BookLeaf
Publishing

Presentation by *BookLeaf Publishing*

Web: www.bookleafpub.com

E-mail: info@bookleafpub.com

ISBN: 9789395756334

First edition 2022

# DEDICATION

For Cody and Oakley

# ACKNOWLEDGEMENT

Thank you to all my friends and family for putting up with my poetry for so long.

# Little Coffee Shop Poem

Here we are
The lonely ones
To the others
We are the lonely ones
But we watch you
Us lonely ones
We sip our coffee and eat our cake
No one judging us
We are the lonely ones
We hear you chat and watch what you say
Not us, the lonely ones
I wonder if you are more lonely then me.

# #firstworldproblems

Sipping coffee, people watching, music playing,
Facebook not working
First world problems

Sipping dirty water, people crying, guns and
bombs sounding, loved ones dying
Real world problems

# If Love is This

Softly shaken and minds merged
My heart left hidden and untouched
Pulls hard and breaks my ribs
Unheard, this deepest sin is clutched.

Beyond the forbidden walls
Away is where I wish to go
Far from your trembling voice and scars
I have dug my heart up from below.

If love is this, I know not what
The earthly spirits purge
Into my soul to grab this heart
Again, and from my broken bones emerge.

Hungry and full of guilt
I long to feel the pain
Of broken hearts I know have felt
Love and long to again.

# Happiness

Happiness is a state in which the smile lies
Far beneath the euphoric tide
A drug induced by a hopeful mind
A faithful mask behind which we hide.

# Nobody Knows You Like I Do

Nobody knows you like I do.
They will think that they know best – they have
done it all before.
But nobody knows you like I do.

I know your cry
I know your laugh
I know your eyes – tired eyes
I know your needs
What nobody else sees.

Nobody knows you like I do.

I know your smile
I know your look
I know your call
I know you.
What nobody else sees.

Nobody knows you like I do.

# I Can't Write Poetry

I try and I try
The reply is the same
-'This isn't the poem we're looking for'
I try old fashioned and pretty
Modern and real
But again and again
-'Sorry, but no'
I try rhyming, I try to not
I find it so hard to stop
I'm starting to lose the plot…
-'Read our suggested poems'
They say
-'Be more like them'
I can't write poetry
Not like that
Not like those forward thinking, award winning,
bone chilling, confessionalists.

# Comfort Of The Storm

I am strangely comforted by the dark stormy sky
The threat of thunder and rain warms me
The anticipation of lightning strikes and power
cuts
An innocence reborn with the excitement of
board games by candlelight.

# Crow

Death calls, silent and eerie
I hear my name in the whispers of the wind
Moving mindlessly through the dormant trees
The black crow calls
He speaks of strange things
Of tall tales
And deep dreams.

# Coffee

I'm shaking
Coffee overload
Sitting and picking
At the scabs I told myself to leave alone.
Anxious and irritable
And now my mind is racing
My stomach is aching
With all the worries I should leave behind
Put to the back of my mind
Bury deep
Close my eyes and sleep
If the coffee lets me.

# An Investigation

A cold air, with a chilling sorrow.
The shore rose over rocks blocking its path.
In the early morning light, a red glow highlights
the scene.
A warning of tears to come.
The sand, crude and harsh, blew up in the air.
I cover my face, but keep moving against the
wind.
Birds cry; no sweet song for me.
I stop, and shiver, and stare.
Blink.
And stare.
Alone, the body is a silhouette of a man no
longer possessed by a troubled consciousness.
Against a fiery glow, it's as if he is entering hell.
But he is already gone.
Whether his soul has gone to a heavenly grave
or an eternal nothingness, I do not know. I do
not wonder.
This is no time for philosophical thought.
This is time for a logical mind.

# A Walk Home (The Deception)

I stand on the pavement
Far from the grass
A white sparkle catches my eye
A pure white seemingly silk shape lies near a tree

I move closer
It looks like a flower
I move closer still
It becomes a rose

I imagine the sweet fragrance
The soft petal in my fingers
I walk closer and kneel down

The rose is nothing more
Than a scrunched up receipt.

# Smoke

Staring at the light
Hiding in the smoke
Wanting to be true but deceiving myself
Becoming my worst enemy
Hypocritical
Becoming the bad memories I once repressed

Maybe the false is what I crave?
This farce is taking over
Knowing that it's wrong, so why carry on?

Listening to sad songs
Forever in my mind from dawn til dusk
Do I crave this morbid feeling?
This melancholy rush?

This smoke I hide in fills my lungs
Becomes the air I breathe, a polluted life-force
A clouded memory, a mixed up mind,
Losing the light
A dirt-filled nonsense is all that remains
As my childhood security fades.

# Willow Skeletons

Willow Skeletons
Hitting the river mirror
In the midnight glow
Images gleam far below

A feeling in the wind
Long forgotten sins
Returning to intertwine
In a star-filled night.

# Nightmares

Some may cry
Others fall still
Sense is like a feather just passing them by

They feel alone
Yet lost in a crowd
All meaning is lost
Every feeling is left to die

Hope is what they yearn
But they do not let it out
Tension is released through painful means

Trust is gone
All friends seem forgotten
Do they have peace in their deepest dreams?

# Nail Polish

I paint my nails
To stop me from biting
Not a bright colour
Just a clear coating
To make them appear glossy
So I leave them alone

Then in the night
When I struggle to sleep
Darkness surrounds
So I cannot see
The shiny polish
I painted to stop me.

# My Little One

He sleeps by my side
And I realise
I made this beautiful boy

His tiny hands and feet
His curly, golden blonde locks
His plumped out lips
His little button nose
And that small dimple that appears with his
smile

I kept you safe
I kept you warm
I loved you from the start
And will forever, with all my heart.

# Forest Walks

Light beams shine through branches intertwined
I walked this path long ago
In my youth, searching to find
A sense of peace, and release from this woe

The dry leaves crunch beneath my feet
Is autumn arriving too soon?
Green leaves still cover me overhead
Turning golden against the sun at noon

Milk thistle seeds float gently by
Spinning and flowing like fairies in dance
Whispering and greeting each other anon
Watching, I stop and gaze almost in a trance

In this moment, I am taken back
To a childlike mind
Searching to find
The path I walked long ago.

# All In My Mind

Everything is out of focus
I've become old and a child over night
Living in the moment
Too hopeless to see the future
Too ashamed to remember the past
Stuck in a clouded bubble
Not part of the world
And the world isn't part of me
There is a storm behind my eyes that I can't hold
back
An iceberg in my throat that I can't hold down
A stabbing in my chest and broken glass in my
head
This is all in my mind
And I can't escape.

# People Watching

Under cover, content and  warm
Cupping my coffee, I am torn
Between watching and listening to stories told
Or contemplating becoming old

I choose the former to distance myself
From my own failings and regret
And try to uncover those of these strangers
instead

Should I look to the old man sitting alone with
his tea
Or the young couple arguing about which film to
see
The tired mum breaking biscuits while nursing
her baby
Or the teen group of girls with their trendy
frappes

I notice a woman at the door
Alone like me
She clumsily pushes through, bags in one hand
In the other, phone and keys

She orders an Americano

No milk, no sugar
Takes a seat in a corner
And opens her phone

I consider that she
Is browsing social media
I like to think that I am more connected to the
world
But really we are both just people watching
Looking for a life more interesting than our own.

# Drunk

In a drunken haze
I am falling
Sinking
Into these quilted sheets
Down into my imaginary rabbit hole
Where there is no one else but me.

# Remember

I don't always remember to take my pills
It can leave me feeling quite ill
I forget to drink enough water in the day
And can't recall all of what I say
I will search my memory for any clues
To where those documents are that I always lose

But I overthink the stupid mistakes I made long
ago when I struggle to sleep
They do not matter now and never really did

And I always remember to tell you good night,
and I love you

Please don't ever forget that I do.